Diplomacy Arabic

Books in the series

edinburghuniversitypress.com/series/emev

● Essential Middle Eastern Vocabularies ●

Diplomacy Arabic

Elisabeth Kendall &
Yehia A. Mohamed

EDINBURGH
University Press

Edinburgh University Press is one of the leading university presses in the UK. We publish academic books and journals in our selected subject areas across the humanities and social sciences, combining cutting-edge scholarship with high editorial and production values to produce academic works of lasting importance. For more information visit our website: edinburghuniversitypress.com

Edinburgh University Press Ltd
The Tun – Holyrood Road
12 (2f) Jackson's Entry
Edinburgh EH8 8PJ

Typeset in Times New Roman and
printed and bound in Great Britain

A CIP record for this book is available from the British Library

ISBN 978 1 4744 6123 8 (hardback)
ISBN 978 1 4744 6124 5 (paperback)
ISBN 978 1 4744 6125 2 (webready PDF)
ISBN 978 1 4744 6126 9 (epub)

CONTENTS

USER GUIDE

To enhance your ability to recall the vocabulary and to pronounce it correctly, this book is accompanied by audio recordings of the entire contents of each chapter, recorded in both English and Arabic. The audio recordings can be downloaded from our website and are compatible with iPods and other devices.

To access the audio files, please follow the instructions on our website: https://edinburghuniversitypress.com/book-diplomacy-arabic.html

Audio recordings

Main features
- Each Arabic term is recorded with authentic native pronunciation at normal speed.
- Each Arabic term is preceded by its equivalent in English.
- Each chapter is recorded as a single MP3 track (the track numbers correspond to the chapter numbers, e.g. Track 01 = Chapter 1).
- The audio files can be played on any MP3-compatible device, enabling you to study on the move.

Tips
- Make sure that you engage actively with the audio recordings by repeating each Arabic term during the pause.
- Pause the recording and challenge yourself to produce the Arabic word before it is announced.

INTRODUCTION

Diplomacy in and on the Arabic-speaking world is now more urgent than ever, following an upsurge in conflict over the past decade. This book aims to provide not only diplomats and others in the diplomatic corps, but also students of international relations and diplomacy with an up-to-date list of the most common terminology and expressions required to communicate and succeed in the field. It does not claim to be exhaustive. Rather, it provides a 'quick-fix' of diplomacy-related vocabulary that includes many recent expressions not found in standard Arabic dictionaries. It contains the key terms essential to anyone seeking to practise, follow or analyse diplomatic efforts between Arabic and English.

The book has ten thematically organised chapters: General; Concepts & Practices; Diplomatic Service & Protocol; Organisations; Elections & Government; Negotiations; Treaties & Agreements; Conflict Resolution & Defence; Civil Society & Human Rights; and Globalisation & Economic Development. Each chapter is internally ordered according to semantic field. For example, the chapter on 'Negotiations' includes sections on types of negotiations, the players involved in negotiations, and the process of negotiating. The book also includes an alphabetised English index to help readers locate relevant vocabulary with ease.

The vocabulary is derived primarily from authentic materials in the field of diplomacy and international relations. The terms were then cross-checked for frequency using ArabiCorpus, a creation of Dilworth Parkinson, Professor of Arabic at Brigham Young University, and by using 'advanced search' options in Arabic on internet search engines.

The book can be utilised by readers as either a comprehensive vocabulary reference guide or an active study tool to develop their discipline-specific vocabulary. Readers can choose to work through the whole book or to focus only on the topics closest to their specific needs.

Repetition has for the most part been avoided. Occasionally, however, the same term appears more than once in the book, where it was deemed germane to more than one chapter.

Notes on the formal presentation

The Arabic is vocalised to ensure correct pronunciation and entrench in the mind the vocalisation patterns of certain structures. However, short vowels are not supplied where

- a fatha precedes a long alif or a ta' marbuta
- a kasra precedes a long ya
- a damma precedes a long waw

End vowels have not been supplied.

Except in compound expressions, most definite articles have been omitted for purposes of simplicity.

However, note that definite articles are required in Arabic in many instances where they are omitted in English (e.g. generic nouns).

In general, Arabic nouns are supplied in both the singular and plural; the plural is printed after the comma. For masculine and feminine sound plurals, the stem word is not repeated; only the plural suffix is noted after a dash.

First form verbs
These have been supplied in the form of the basic stem (past tense masculine singular) followed by the present tense (masculine singular with the middle vowel marked) and the masdar (verbal noun). The middle vowel of the past tense has only been supplied where this is *not* a fatha. Where two short vowels are marked with the same letter, this indicates that both are possible.

Derived forms of the verb
These have been supplied only in the form of the basic stem (past tense masculine singular), since present tense vocalisation and masdars are predictable for derived forms of the verb. The present tense and masdars have been supplied only where the spelling of the verb changes significantly (for example, the present tense of second form first radical hamza verbs), where a separate vocabulary item is intended, or where the word is commonly misvocalised.

1. GENERAL

الدِّبْلوماسيّة \ مَجال الدِّبْلوماسيّة	diplomacy
دِبْلوماسيّ	diplomat/diplomatic
السِّلْك الدِّبْلوماسيّ	the diplomatic corps
الهَيْئة الدِّبْلوماسيّة	the diplomatic service
بْروتُوكول (الأُصُول والأَعْراف الدِّبْلوماسيّة)	protocol
عَلاقات دِبْلوماسيّة	diplomatic relations/ties
جُهود دِبْلوماسيّة	diplomatic efforts
حَصانة دِبْلوماسيّة	diplomatic immunity
تَمْثيل دِبْلوماسيّ	diplomatic representation
مُراسَلات	correspondence
إعْتِماد	accreditation
سَفير، سُفَراء	ambassador
سِفارة، ـات	embassy
قُنْصُل، قَناصِلة	consul
قُنْصُليّة، ـات	consulate

مَنْدوب، ـ ون	delegate
العَلاقات الدَّوليّة	international relations (IR)
الشُّؤُون الدَّوليّة	international/foreign affairs
السِّياسة الدَّوليّة	international/global policy
السِّياسة الخارِجيّة	foreign policy
المُجْتَمع الدَّوليّ	the international community
على الصَّعِيد الدَّوليّ	at the international level
مُؤَسَّسات دوليّة	international institutions
النِّظام العالَميّ \ الدَّوليّ	the international order
القانون الدَّوليّ	international law
تَعاوُن دَوليّ	international cooperation/collaboration
مَوْقِف دَوليّ، مَواقِف دوَليّة	international position
قَرار دَوليّ، ـات دَوليّة	international resolution
مَساعٍ دوَليّة	international endeavours
مَبْدأ، مَبادِئ	principle/doctrine
مَبْدأ مونرو	Monroe Doctrine

وِزارة الخارِجِيّة	State Department
وِزارة الشُّؤُون الخارِجِيّة	Ministry of Foreign Affairs
صِراع، ـات	conflict
نِزاع، ـات	dispute
نُشُوب \ اِنْدِلاع الحَرب	outbreak of war
تَوَتُّر، ـات	tension
إسْتِعْمار	colonisation
إسْتِعْمارِيّة	colonialism
إحْتِلال	occupation
حِصار	blockade/embargo
عُقُوبات دَوْلِيّة	international sanctions
تَحْكِيم دَوْلِيّ	international arbitration
تَطْبِيع	naturalisation/normalisation
هُدْنة	truce
لاجِئ، لاجِئُون	refugee
لُجُوء سِياسِيّ	political asylum
تَفاوَض	to negotiate

مُفاوَضات	negotiations
مُباحَثات	discussions
مُحادَثات	talks
مُؤْتَمَر، ‑ات	conference
جَلْسة، جَلَسات	panel
إسْتِشارة \ مُشاوَرة \ تَشاوُر، ‑ات	consultation
مُعاهَدة، ‑ات	treaty
مُعاهدة السَّلام	peace treaty
إتِّفاق \ إتِّفاقِيّة، ‑ات	agreement/convention
عَقْد، عُقُود	contract
مِيثاق، مَواثيق	charter/pact/compact
مِيثاق الأُمَم المُتَّحِدة	UN Charter
وَثيقة، وَثائِق	document/instrument
مُذَكِّرة، ‑ات	memorandum
بَيان، ‑ات	announcement
تَصْريح، ‑ات	statement
إعْلان، ‑ات	declaration

إِقْتِراح، ـات	motion
هَيْئة، ـات	body/entity
مُؤَسَّسة، ـات	institution
مُنَظَّمة، ـات	organisation
حِلْف \ تَحالُف	alliance
مَقَرّ، ـات	headquarters/premises
مَقَرّ دائِم	permanent headquarters
العالَم العَرَبِيّ	the Arab world
الأُمّة العَرَبِيّة	the Arab community/nation
العالَم الإسْلامِيّ	the Islamic world
الأُمّة الإسْلامِيّة	the Islamic community/ummah
الشَّرْق الأَوْسَط	the Middle East
القَوْمِيّة \ الوَطَنِيّة	nationalism
حُدُود دَوَلِيّة	international boundaries/borders
صاحِب \ صاحِبة الفَخامة	His/Her Excellency (HE)
صاحِب \ صاحِبة الجَلالة	His/Her Majesty (HM)

صاحِب \ صاحِبة السُمُو المَلَكيّ	His/Her Royal Highness (HRH)
سُمُو الأَمِير \ الأَمِيرة	His/Her Highness Prince/Princess
سَعادة السَّفِير \ السّفِيرة	His/Her Excellency Ambassador (HE Ambassador)

2. CONCEPTS & PRACTICES

شَعْبَوِيّة \ شَعْبِيّة	populism
لِيبْرالِيّة	liberalism
لِيبْرالِيّة جَدِيدة	neo-liberalism
مُحافَظة	conservatism
مُحافَظة جَدِيدة	neo-conservativism (neo-con)
إِشْتِراكِيّة	socialism
شُمولِيّة	totalitarianism
شُيوعِيّة	communism
ماركِسِيّة	Marxism
رَأْسْمالِيّة	capitalism
إِنْفِصالِيّة	separatism
إِنْعِزالِيّة	isolationism
قَبَلِيّة	tribalism
مَذْهَبِيّة \ طائِفِيّة	sectarianism
فِئَوِيّة	factionalism
تَطَرُّف	extremism

نازِيّة جَديدة	neo-Nazism
مُعاداة السامِيّة	anti-semitism
صَهْيونِيّة	Zionism
أُصولِيّة	fundamentalism
نُخْبَوِيّة	elitism
عُنْصُرِيّة	racism
تَعَدُّدِيّة	pluralism
إنْتِهازِيّة	opportunism
واقِعِيّة	realism
عَقْلانِيّة	rationalism
ما بَعْد الحَداثة	postmodernism
يوتوبِيّة \ مِثالِيّة	utopianism
مَكْيافيلِيّة	Machiavellianism
تَدَرُّج	incrementalism
دُسْتورِيّة	constitutionalism
مَلَكِيّة	monarchism
مَلَكِيّة دُسْتورِيّة	constitutional monarchy

حُكْم ذاتيّ	self-rule/autonomy
حُكْم لا مَرْكَزيّ	decentralised rule
سُلْطة مُطْلَقة	absolute power
سِيادة	sovereignty
نَظَرِيّة الدَّوَلِيّة	theory of international politics
نَظَرِيّة المَدْرَسة الإنْجِليزيّة في العَلاقات الدَّوَلِيّة	English School of international relations theory
نَظَرِيّة الوَكيل الرَّئيسيّ (بَين المُوَكِّل والوَكيل)	principal-agent theory
فِعْل ـ رَدّ فِعْل	action-reaction
عامِل ـ بُنْية	agent-structure
نَظَرِيّة الألْعاب	game theory
هَيْمَنة	hegemony
نَظَرِيّة الإسْتِقْرار المُهَيْمِن	hegemonic stability theory
نَظَرِيّة التَّقارُب (الإلْتِقاء عِنْدَ نُقْطة واحِدة)	convergence theory

تَحْلِيل إِلَى عَوامِل	factor analysis
نَمُوذَج \ مِثال \ نَمَط	paradigm
وَضع السِّياسات	policymaking
دِبْلوماسيّة تَقْلِيدِيّة	traditional diplomacy
دِبْلوماسيّة عَلَنِيّة	public diplomacy
دِبْلوماسيّة ثُنائِيّة	bilateral diplomacy
دِبْلوماسيّة مُتَعَدِّدة الأَطْراف	multilateral diplomacy
دِبْلوماسيّة شَعْبِيّة	popular diplomacy
دِبْلوماسيّة هادِئة	quiet diplomacy
دِبْلوماسيّة صارِمة	firm diplomacy
دِبْلوماسيّة نَشِطة	active diplomacy
دِبْلوماسيّة القِمّة	summit diplomacy
دِبْلوماسيّة المُؤْتَمَرات	conference diplomacy
دِبْلوماسيّة مُتَجَوِّلة	ambulatory diplomacy
دِبْلوماسيّة مَكّوكِيّة	shuttle diplomacy
دِبْلوماسيّة سِرّيّة	secret diplomacy
دِبْلوماسيّة تَرابُطِيّة	associative diplomacy

دِبْلوماسيّة وِقائيّة — preventive diplomacy

سياسة بيرُوقْراطِيّة — bureaucratic politics

سياسة عُلْيا — high politics

سياسة الإحْتِواء — containment policy

مُتَمَسِّك بالقانون والأخْلاق — legalistic-moralistic

مُشارَكة إيْجابيّة — constructive engagement

الحَدّ من الأضْرار — damage limitation

مَناطِق السِّلْم — zones of peace

مَناطِق الإضْطِرابات — zones of turmoil

تَرابُط مُعَقَّد — complex interdependence

تَساوي الدُّوَل — equality of states

وِصاية — trusteeship

تَقارُب — rapprochement

تَطْبيع — normalisation

الحَصانة خارِج حُدُود الإقْليم — extraterritoriality

سِيادة — sovereignty

شَرْعِيّة	legitimacy
حِيادِيّة	neutralism
وَساطة	mediation
تَبادُل	reciprocity
إعْتِراف	recognition
حِفْظ السِّلْم	peacekeeping
حِماية المَصالِح	protection of interests
الوَضْع الرّاهِن	the status quo
لا شَيء دُونَ مُقابِل	nothing for nothing
تَوازُن القُوّة	balance of power
مَبْدأ التَّبَعِيّة \ مَبْدأ تَفْريع السُّلْطة	subsidiarity principle
إسْتِقْطاب	polarisation
إعْلان مَبادِئ	declaration of principles
قَنَوات دِبْلوماسِيّة	diplomatic channels
طُرُق دِبْلوماسِيّة	diplomatic methods
مَصْدَر دِبْلوماسِيّ	diplomatic source

صِفة المُراقِب observer status

دَوائِر دِبْلوماسِيّة diplomatic circles

رَوابِط دِبْلوماسِيّة diplomatic connections

قِسْم رِعاية المَصالِح interests section

دَوْلة مُضِيفة host nation

إتِّفاق المَقَرّ headquarters agreement

دَوْلة حاجِزة buffer state

نِظام عالَميّ جَديد new world order

حُكُومة عالَمِيّة world government

نِظام أُحادِي القُطْب unipolarity

عَلاقات ثُنائِيّة
(المُفاوَضات حَول
السّياسة الخارِجِيّة
بين طَرَفَين) bilateralism

ثُنائِيّة المَحاوِر bipolar

القانُون الدَّوْلِيّ العُرْفِيّ customary international law

عُرْف دِبْلوماسِيّ diplomatic norm

إقامة عَلاقات
دِبْلوماسِيّة establishment of diplomatic
relations

أوُراق الإعْتِماد	credentials
خِطاب الإعْتِماد	letter of credentials
تَبادُل السُّفَراء	exchange of ambassadors
إستِئناف العَلاقات الدِّبْلوماسِيّة	resumption of diplomatic relations
إستِدْعاء السَّفير	recalling the ambassador
إستِدْعاء السَّفير للتَّشاوُر	consultation
خَفْض مُسْتَوى التَّمْثيل الدِّبْلوماسيّ	lowering diplomatic representation
رَفْع مُسْتَوى التَّمْثيل الدِّبْلوماسيّ	upgrading diplomatic representation
تَجْميد العَلاقات الدِّبْلوماسيّة	freezing diplomatic relations
قَطْع العَلاقات الدِّبْلوماسيّة	severing diplomatic relations
وُجوب مُغادَرة البِلاد خِلال يَوْم واحِد	obligation to leave the country within a day
مُعامَلة بالمِثْل	reciprocity
مَساعٍ دِبْلوماسِيّة	diplomatic demarches
مَساعٍ حَميدة	good offices

جُهود دِبْلوماسِيّة	diplomatic efforts
حُسْن الجِوار	bon voisinage/good neighbourliness
إعْتِراف دِبْلوماسِيّ	diplomatic recognition
تَمْثيل دِبْلوماسِيّ	diplomatic representation
إتِّصالات دِبْلوماسِيّة	diplomatic contacts
وَضْع دِبْلوماسِيّ	diplomatic status
خُطُوات دِبْلوماسِيّة	diplomatic steps
تأييد دِبْلوماسِيّ	diplomatic support
تَحَرُّك دِبْلوماسِيّ	diplomatic move
نَشاط دِبْلوماسِيّ	diplomatic action
حَمْلة دِبْلوماسِيّة	diplomatic campaign
رَدّ دِبْلوماسِيّ	diplomatic response
صَمْت دِبْلوماسِيّ	diplomatic silence
أزْمة دِبْلوماسِيّة	diplomatic crisis

3. DIPLOMATIC SERVICE & PROTOCOL

السِّلْك الدِّبْلوماسيّ	diplomatic corps
مُوَظَّفُو السِّلْك الدِّبْلوماسيّ	diplomatic staff
رَئيس البَعْثة الدِّبْلوماسيّة	head of mission
عَميْد السِّلْك الدِّبْلوماسيّ	dean of the diplomatic corps
كِبار الشَّخْصيّات والمَسْؤولِين أصْحاب المَقام الرَّفِيْع	dignitaries
سَفير، سُفَراء	ambassador
تَعْيين	appointment
سَفير مُعْتَمَد	accredited ambassador
تَقْديم أوْراق الإعْتِماد	presentation of credentials
على مُسْتَوَى السُّفَراء	at ambassador level
مَنْدُوب فَوْق العادة	envoy extraordinary/ special envoy

حامِل الحَقيبة الدِّبْلوماسِيّة	diplomatic courier
القائِم المُؤَقَّت بِأَعْمال السِّفارة	chargé d'affaires ad interim
سِفارة	embassy
مَقَرّ السِّفارة	embassy premises
مَقَرّ إقامة السَّفير \ مَنْزِل السَّفير	ambassador's residence
مُتَحَدِّث بِاسْم السِّفارة	embassy spokesman
مُسْتَشار السِّفارة	embassy chancellor
سِكْرتير أَوّل	first secretary
القُنْصُلِيّة	consulate
مَكْتَب قُنْصُلِيّ	consular office
السِّلْك القُنْصُلِيّ	consular service
عَمِيد السِّلْك القُنْصُلِيّ	dean of the consular corps
قُنْصُل	consul
نائِب القُنْصُل	vice-consul
مُوَظَّف قُنْصُلِيّ	consular officer

مُلْحَق ثَقافِيّ	cultural attaché
مُلْحَق عَسْكَرِيّ	military attaché
مُلْحَق تِجارِيّ	commercial attaché
إِنْضَمَّ إلى السِّلْك الدِّبْلوماسِيّ	to join the diplomatic corps
دَخَلَ الهَيْئة الدِّبْلوماسِيّة	to enter the diplomatic service
إعْفاء	exemption
إِمْتِياز، ـات	privilege
حَصانة، ـات	immunity
بِرتوكول	protocol
مَراسِم	ceremony/protocol
مُدير المَراسِم \ التَّشْريفات	chief of protocol
أعْراف وأُصُول دِبْلوماسِيّة	diplomatic etiquette
إجْراءات بِرُوتُوكُولِيّة	protocol procedures
تَرْتيبات	arrangements
إسْتِعْدادات	preparations

زِيارة رَسْمِيّة	state visit
بَرْنامَج زيارة رَسْمِيّة	the agenda for a state visit
إسْتِقْبال الوُفُود	welcoming delegates
إسْتِقْبال السُّفَراء الجُدُد	welcoming new ambassadors
جَواز دِبْلوماسِيّ	diplomatic passport
قَواعِد المُجامَلة	courtesy
حُسْن السُّلُوك	good conduct
أَسْبَقِيّة	precedence
تَراتُبِيّة	hierarchy
لَقَب، ألْقاب	title
فَخامة	Excellency (president)
مَعالِي \ سَعادة	Excellency (ambassador or cabinet minister)
سِيادة	Excellency
فَضيلة \ سَماحة	Eminence (Muslim cleric)
غِبْطة \ قَداسة	Beatitude/Holiness (Christian cleric)
المُحْتَرَم	Honourable

هَيْبة \ إعْتِبار	prestige
صيغة المُخاطَبة	form of address
قَواعِد اللِّباس	dress code
دَعْوة دِبْلوماسِيّة	diplomatic invitation
حُضُور المُناسَبات وحَفَلات الإسْتِقبال	attending events and receptions
تَرتيب الجُلُوس إلى الطّاوِلة	planning table seating
مَراسِم الإسْتقبال	receiving line
آداب المائِدة	table manners
قَدَّم النَّخْب	to give the toast
لُغة دِبْلوماسِيّة	diplomatic language
مَهارات دِبْلوماسِيّة	diplomatic skills

4. ORGANISATIONS

مُنَظَّمة، ـات	organisation
هَيْئة، ـات	body/entity
مُؤَسَّسة، ـات	institution
كِيان، ـات	entity
رابِطة، رَوابِط	association/league
جَماعة، ـات	group/community
مَجْمُوعة، ـات	group
جَمْعِيّة، ـات	assembly/society
تَجَمُّع، ـات	gathering/assembly/caucus
مُجْتَمع، ـات	society
حَرَكة، ـات	movement
تَيّار، ـات	current
مُنْتَدى، مُنْتَدَيات	forum
جِهاز، أَجْهِزة	organ
وَكالة، ـات	agency
مَعْهَد، مَعاهِد	institute

مُفَوَّضيّة، ـات	commission/office/legation
سِلْك \ هَيْئة	corps
جِلْف، أَحْلاف	alliance/pact
إتِّحاد، ـات	union/federation
تَحالُف، ـات	alliance/coalition
إئْتِلاف، ـات	coalition/consortium
كُتْلة، كُتَل	bloc
مِحْوَر، مَحاوِر	axis
نِقابة، ـات	syndicate/union
مَجْلِس، مَجالِس	council
لَجْنة، لِجان	commission
بَرْنامَج، بَرامِج	programme
مَشْرُوع، مَشاريع	project
هَيْكَل، هَياكِل	structure
خُطّة، خُطَط	scheme/plan
صُنْدُوق، صَناديق	fund
مُنَظّمة الأُمَم المُتَّحِدة	United Nations Organization (UN)

الجَمْعِيّة العامّة	General Assembly
مَجْلِس الأَمْن	Security Council
المَجْلِس الاقْتِصاديّ والاجْتِماعيّ	Economic and Social Council
مَجْلِس الوصاية	Trusteeship Council
مَحْكَمة العَدْل الدّوَلِيّة	International Court of Justice (ICJ)
الأَمانة العامّة	Secretariat
الأَمِين العامّ	Secretary-General
صُنْدُوق الأُمَم المُتَّحِدة	United Nations fund
صُنْدُوق النقد الدّوَلِي	International Monetary Fund (IMF)
البَنْك الدّوَلِي	World Bank
البَنْك الدّوَلِي للإِنْشاء والتَّعْمِير	International Bank for Reconstruction and Development
صُنْدُوق الأُمَم المُتَّحِدة للطُّفولة (اليونيسيف)	United Nations Children's Fund (UNICEF)
بَرْنامَج الأُمَم المُتَّحِدة للتَّنْمية	United Nations Development Programme (UNDP)

بَرْنامَج الأُمَم المُتَّحِدة لِلْبِيئة	United Nations Environment Programme (UNEP)
الهَيْئة الحُكُومِيّة الدَّوْلِيّة المَعْنِيّة بِتَغَيُّر المَناخ	Intergovernmental Panel on Climate Change (IPCC)
مُنَظَّمة الأغذِية والزِّراعة لِلأُمَم المُتَّحِدة (الفاو)	Food and Agriculture Organization (FAO)
بَرْنامَج الأغْذِية العالَمِيّ	World Food Programme (WFP)
الصُّنْدُوق الدَّوَلِيّ لِلْتَنْمِية الزِّراعِيّة (إيفاد)	International Fund for Agricultural Development (IFAD)
مُنَظَّمة الصِّحة العالَمِيّة	World Health Organization (WHO)
مُنَظَّمة العَمَل الدَّوَلِيّة	International Labour Organization (ILO)
مُنَظَّمة التِّجارة العالَمِيّة	World Trade Organization (WTO)
غُرْفة التِّجارة الدَّوَلِيّة	International Chamber of Commerce (ICC)
صُنْدُوق الأُمَم المُتَّحِدة لِلسُّكّان	United Nations Population Fund (UNPF)

مُنَظَّمة الأُمَم المُتَّحِدة لِلتَّربية والعُلُوم والثَّقافة (اليونيسكو)	UN Educational, Scientific and Cultural Organization (UNESCO)
المُفَوَّضية السّامية للأُمَم المُتَّحِدة لِشُؤُون اللاجِئين	UN Refugee Agency (UNHCR)
وَكالة الأُمَم المُتَّحِدة لإغاثة وتَشغِيل اللاجِئين الفِلَسْطينيّين (الأونروا)	United Nations Relief and Works Agency for Palestine Refugees (UNRWA)
اللَّجْنة الدَّوَلِيّة للصَّلِيب الأَحمر	International Committee of the Red Cross (ICRC)
صُنْدُوق الأُمَم المُتَّحِدة الإنْمائيّ لِلْمَرأة	United Nations Development Fund for Women (UNDFW)
المُنَظَّمة الدَّوَلِيّة للهِجرة	International Organization for Migration (IOM)
مُنَظَّمة العَفُو الدَّوَلِيّة	Amnesty International
مُفَوَّضية الأُمَم المُتَّحِدة السّامية لِحُقُوق الإنْسان	United Nations High Commission for Human Rights (UNHCR)

عَمَليّات الأُمَم المُتَّحِدة لِحِفظ السَّلام	United Nations peacekeeping operations
قُوَّات الأُمَم المُتَّحِدة لِحِفظ السَّلام	United Nations Peacekeeping Forces
الوكالة الدَّوليّة للطّاقة الذَّرّيّة	International Atomic Energy Agency (IAEA)
مُنَظَّمة حَظر الأَسْلِحة الكِيْمِيائيّة	Organization for the Prohibition of Chemical Weapons (OPCW)
اللَّجْنة التَّحْضيرية لمُنَظَّمة مُعاهَدة الحَظْر الشّامِل للتَّجارِب النَّوَويّة	Preparatory Commission for the Comprehensive Nuclear-Test-Ban Treaty Organization (CTBTO)
لَجْنة نَزْع السِّلاح	Disarmament Commission
مَحكَمة العَدْل الدَّوَليّة	International Court of Justice (ICJ)
المَحكَمة الجِنائيّة الدَّوَليّة	International Criminal Court (ICC)
لَجْنة القانون الدَّوَليّ	International Law Commission
الإتِّحاد الأُوُرُوبيّ	European Union (EU)

مَجْلِس أُورُوبا	Council of Europe
حِلْف شَمال الأطْلَسيّ (الناتو)	North Atlantic Treaty Organization (NATO)
رابِطة التِّجارة الحُرّة الأوروبيّة	European Free Trade Association (EFTA)
الإتِّحاد من أجْل المُتَوَسِّط	Union for the Mediterranean (UfM)
دُوَل الكُومُنولْث	Commonwealth
مَجْمُوعة العِشْرين	Group of 20 (G20)
مَجْمُوعة الدُّوَل الصِّناعيّة الثُّمانيّة	Group of Eight (G8)
مَجْمُوعة الدُّوَل السَّبْعة	Group of Seven (G7)
مُنَظَّمة الدُّوَل المُصَدِّرة لِلْبَتْرُول (أوبك)	Organization of the Petroleum Exporting Countries (OPEC)
البُلْدان غَيْر الأعْضاء في أوبك	non-OPEC countries
جامِعة الدُّوَل العَرَبيّة	League of Arab States (LAS)
مُنَظَّمة التَّعاوُن الإسْلاميّ	The Organization of Islamic Cooperation (OIC)

المُنَظَّمة الإسلاميّة للتَّرْبيّة والعُلُوم والثَّقافة	The Islamic Educational, Scientific and Cultural Organization (IESCCO)
مَجْلِس التَّعاوُن لِدُوَل الخَلِيج العَرَبِي \ مَجْلِس التَّعاوُن الخَلِيْجيّ	Gulf Cooperation Council (GCC)
إتِّحاد المَغْرِب العَرَبيّ	Arab Maghreb Union (AMU)
الإتِّحاد الإفْريقيّ	African Union (AU)
تَجَمُّع دُوَل السّاحِل والصَّحْراء	The Community of Sahelo-Saharan States (CEN-SAD)
السُّوْق المُشْتَرَكة لِدُوَل شَرْق إفْريقيا والجَنُوب الإفْريقيّ (كوميسا)	The Common Market for Eastern and Southern Africa (COMESA)
الإتِّحاد النَّقْدِي لِدُوَل غَرْب إفْريقيا	The Economic Community of West African States (ECOWAS)
رابِطة جَنُوب آسْيا للتَّعاوُن الإقْليميّ	The South Asia Association for Regional Cooperation (SAARC)
رابِطة دُوَل جَنُوب شَرْق آسْيا (أسْيان)	Association of Southeast Asia Nations (ASEAN)

مُنْتَدَى جُزُر المُحِيط الهادِئ	Pacific Islands Forum (PIF)
مَجْمُوعة دُوَل أَمْرِيكا اللّاتِينِيّة والكارِيبِيّ	The Latin American and Caribbean Group (GRULAC)
إتِّحاد الجُمْهُوريات السُّوفِيتِيّة \ الإتِّحاد السُّوفيتيّ	Soviet Union
حَرَكِة عَدَم الإنْحِياز	Non-Aligned Movement (NAM)

5. ELECTIONS & GOVERNMENT

اِنْتِخاب، ـات	election
اِنْتِخابات عامّة	general elections
اِنْتِخابات فيدراليّة	federal elections
اِنْتِخابات فَرْعيّة	by-elections
اِنْتِخابات رِئاسيّة	presidential elections
اِنْتِخابات مَحَلّيّة	local elections
اِنْتِخابات التَّجْديد النِصْفيّ	mid-term elections
دَوْرة ثانية لِلْاِنْتِخابات	run-off election (second round)
اِنْتِخابات دَوْرة التَّصْفية الرِّئاسيّة	run-off presidential election
اِنْتِخابات مُبكِّرة	early elections
اِنْتِخابات حُرّة ونَزيهة	free and fair elections
تَمْثيل نِسْبيّ	proportional representation
نِظام أَكْثَريّ	majority system
عَمَليّة اِنْتِخابيّة	electoral process

لَجْنة إِنْتِخابيّة	electoral commission
رَقابة إِنْتِخابيّة	election monitoring
إِسْتِفْتاء	referendum
إِسْتِطْلاع رَأي	opinion poll
الرَأي العامّ	public opinion
إِقْتِراع، ـات	ballot
إِقْتِراع سِرّيّ	secret ballot
صُنْدوق إِقْتِراع	ballot box
مَرْكَز إِقْتِراع	polling station
حَمْلة، حَمَلات	campaign
بَيان إِنْتِخابيّ	election manifesto
مُرَشَّح، ـون	candidate
مُرَشَّح مُسْتقِلّ	independent candidate
شَخْصيّة، ـات	personality
صورة، صُوَر	image
شُهْرة	reputation
إشْتِهار	notoriety
شَعْبيّة	popularity

تَراجُع في الشَعْبِيّة	decline in popularity
إلْغاء التَرْشيح	de-selection
لائِحة حِزْبيّة	party list
وَلاء لِ	loyalty to
الناخِبون	the electorate
مُسَجَّلون في قَوائِم الإقْتِراع	registered voters
سِجِلّ الناخِبين	register of electors
غَيْر الناخِبين	non-voters
إنْتِخابيّ	electoral
لائِحة إنْتِخابيّة	electoral roll
دائِرة إنْتِخابيّة	constituency
مَقْعَد، مَقاعِد	seat
صَوْت، أصْوات	vote
إنْتِصار، ـات	victory
وِلاية ثانية	second term
أغْلَبِيّة مُطْلَقة	absolute majority
بَرْلِمان مُعَلَّق	hung parliament

تَزْوير الإنْتِخابات	election-rigging
تَزْوير الدَوائِر	gerrymandering
شَفَّافِيّة	transparency
عَتَبة، عَتَب \ أعْتاب	threshold
نِسْبة المُشارَكة	turnout
فَرْز الأصْوات	vote count
إعادة فَرْز الأصْوات	re-count
دِعاية	propaganda
أجْرَى إنْتِخابات	to hold elections
أجَّل إنْتِخابات	to postpone elections
ألْغَى إنْتِخابات	to cancel elections
إنْتَخَب	to elect
أعاد الإنْتِخاب	to re-elect
صَوَّت	to vote
أحْجَم عَن	to abstain from
فاز يفوز فَوْز في	to gain/win in
أحْرَز إنْتِصاراً ساحِقاً	to win a landslide victory

أَحْرَزَ أَغْلَبِيّة ساحِقة	to secure an overwhelming majority
وقع يقَع وُقوع في إسْتِطْلاعات الرّأي	to fall in the polls
أخذ يأخُذ أَخْذ أَعِنّة الحُكومة	to take up the reins of government
وصل يصِل وُصول إلى السُّلْطة	to come to power
نَصَّب	to appoint
رَشَّح	to nominate
الحِزْب الدّيمُقْراطيّ	Democratic Party
الحِزْب الجُمْهوريّ	Republican Party
الكونجرس	Congress
مَجْلِس الشُّيوخ	Senate
مَجْلِس النُّوّاب	House of Representatives
بَرْلَمان	Parliament
حِزْب العُمّال	Labour Party
حِزْب المُحافِظين	Conservative Party
الحِزْب الدّيمُقْراطيّ اللّيبْراليّ	Liberal Democrat Party

أَحْزاب اليَمين المُتَطَرِّف	far-right parties
أَحْزاب اليَسار المُتَطَرِّف	far-left parties
حِزْب حاكِم	ruling party
الحِزْب الأَكْثَر اتِّساعاً	the most widespread party
الحِزْب الأَسْرَع نُمُواً	the fastest growing party
نِظام الحِزْبِ الواحِد	one-party system
نِظام الأَحْزابِ المُتَعَدِّدة	multi-party system
حُكومة، ـات	government
تَصْويت عَلَى الثِّقة	vote of confidence
تَصْويت بِسَحْب الثِّقة	vote of no-confidence
حُكومة مُؤَقَّتة	caretaker/interim government
حُكومة انْتِقاليّة	transition government
حُكومة ائْتِلافيّة	coalition government
مَجْلِس الوُزَراء	cabinet
حُكومة ظِلّ	shadow cabinet

تَعْديل وِزاريّ	cabinet reshuffle
سُلْطة مُؤَقَّتة	interim authority
نِظام، أَنْظِمة	regime
رَئيس، رُؤَساء	president
وَزير، وُزَراء	minister
رَئيس الوُزَراء	prime minister
صاحِب المَقام	incumbent
مَنْصِب رِئاسةِ الوُزَراء	the office of prime minister
نائِب، نُوّاب	member of parliament (MP)/deputy
سياسيّ، -ون	politician
قائِد، قُوّاد \ قادة	leader
زَعيم، زُعَماء	leader
ثائِر، ثُوّار	revolutionary
مُتَمَرِّد، -ون	rebel
مُنْشَقّ، -ون	dissident
مُنافِس، -ون	rival

خَصْم، خُصُوم	opponent
مُؤَيِّد، ـون	supporter
مُتَعاطِف، ـون	sympathiser
ناشِط \ مُنَشِّط، ـون	activist
والٍ، وُلاة \ مُحافِظ، ـون	governor
جُمْهوريّة، ـات	republic
دَوْلة، دُوَل	state
وَطَن، أَوْطان	nation
شَعْب، شُعوب	people
بِلاد، بُلْدان	country
دَوْلة قَوْميّة	nation-state
أُمّة	Islamic community/ummah
عاصِمة، عَواصِم	capital
ولاية، ـات	province
مُحافَظة، ـات	governorate
مُديريّة، ـات	district
إِسْتِقْلال	independence

وَحْدة	unity
ثَوْرة، ـات	revolution
إنْقِلاب، ـات	coup
تَغْيير النِظام	regime change
إنْتِفاضة	rebellion/intifadah
مُقاومة	resistance
إحْتِجاج، ـات	protest
مُظاهَرة، ـات	demonstration
مَسيرة	rally/march

6. NEGOTIATIONS

مُفاوَضات	negotiations
تَفاوَض	to negotiate (with one another)
فاوَض	to negotiate (a treaty, etc.)
عمَليّة تَفاوُضيّة	negotiation process
مَوقِف تَفاوُضيّ	negotiating position
مَسار تَفاوُضيّ	negotiation route
تَحفُّظات تَفاوُضيّة	negotiated reservations
مَهارات التَّفاوُض	negotiation skills
قابِل للتَّفاوُض	negotiable
غَيْر قابِل للتَّفاوُض	non-negotiable
مُفاوَضات تَمهيديّة	preliminary negotiations
مُفاوَضات رَسْميّة	official negotiations
مُفاوَضات سِرّيّة	secret negotiations
مُفاوَضات الأبْواب الخَلْفيّة	track 2/backchannel negotiations
مُفاوَضات مَشْروطة	conditional negotiations
مُفاوَضات ثُنائيّة	bilateral negotiations

مُفاوَضات مُتَعَدِّدة الأَطْراف	multilateral negotiations
مُفاوَضات مُباشِرة	direct negotiations
مُفاوَضات غَير مُباشِرة	indirect negotiations
مُفاوَضات مُتَواصِلة	continuous negotiations
مُفاوَضات مُتَعَثِّرة	troubled/stalled negotiations
مُفاوَضات ناجِحة	successful negotiations
مُفاوَضات فاشِلة	failed negotiations
مُستَوى المُفاوَضات	level of negotiations
مُفاوَضات عَلى أَعْلَى مُستَوى	negotiations at the highest level
مَرحَلة المُفاوَضات، مَراحِل المُفاوضات	phase/stage of negotiations
أَساس المُفاوَضات، أُسُس المُفاوَضات	basis of negotiations, bases of negotiations
أَجواء المُفاوَضات	negotiation climate
سَيْر المُفاوَضات	negotiations progress
تَقَدُّم في المُفاوَضات	progress in negotiations

حَقَّقَت \ أَحْرَزَت المُفاوَضات تَقَدُّماً مَلْمُوساً	tangible progress has been made in the negotiations
تَعليق المُفاوَضات	suspension of negotiations
إستِئناف المُفاوَضات	resumption of negotiations
مُواصَلة \ مُتابَعة المُفاوَضات	continuation of negotiations
إيقاف المُفاوَضات	negotiations stoppage
إرْجاء \ تأجيل المُفاوَضات	postponement of negotiations
وَضع جَدوَل الأعْمال	agenda setting
بَدْء الإجْراءات	initiation of the procedure
تَفْويض التَّفاوُض	negotiations mandate
خِطاب نَوايا	letter of intent (LOI)
تَشاوُر	consultation
تَبادُل المُذَكِّرات	exchange of memos
مُذَكِّرة تَفاهُم	memorandum of understanding (MOU)
بِناء التَّوافُق	building consensus

بِناء الثِّقة	building trust
بِناء السَّلام	peacebuilding
القِيَم المُشْتَرَكة	common values
تَنازُل، ـات	concession
تَنازُلات مُتَبادَلة	logrolling
تَضارُب المَصالِح	conflict of interest
إعْداد (تَصْميم) الصَّفْقة	deal design
إجْماع	consensus
بَون شاسِع \ فَجْوة عَميقة	deep gap
صَفَقات خَلْف الكَواليس	backroom deals
تَزايُد الضُّغوط	increase in pressure
جَولة (من الـ) مُفاوَضات	round of negotiations
مُفاوَضات نِهائيّة \ خِتاميّة	final negotiations
بَيان خِتاميّ	concluding statement/ final statement

مُفاوِض، -ون	negotiator
أطْراف التَّفاوُض	negotiating parties
مَنْدوب، -ون	delegate
وَفْد، وُفود	delegation
بَعْثة، بَعَثات	mission
فَوَّض \ وَكَّل	to delegate
عُضو الوَفْد	delegation member
رَئيس الوَفْد	delegation president
وُفود مُشارِكة	participating delegations
النّاطِق بِاسْم الوَفْد	delegation speaker
لَجْنة، لِجان	commission/committee
لَجْنة تابِعة لِلأُمَم المُتَّحِدة	UN commission
عُضو اللَّجنة	commissioner
مَنْدوب مُفوَّض	plenipotentiary
مَنْدوب سامٍ	high commissioner
وَكيل، وُكَلاء	agent
وَكيل رَئيسيّ	principal-agent

مُفاوضون خَلْف الكَواليس	backstage negotiators
لَجْنة المُصالَحة	reconciliation committee
وَسيط، وُسَطاء	mediator
وِساطة	mediation
مُراقِب، -ون	observer
صَلاحِيّات كامِلة لِلتَّفاوُض	full powers of negotiation
تَجاوَز حُدود صَلاحِيّات	to exceed the limits of one's competence
مَوْقِع \ مَكان عَقْد المُفاوَضات	negotiations terrain
طاوِلة المُفاوَضات	negotiations table
طاوِلة مُستَديرة	roundtable
مَنصّة التَّحَدُّث	floor/platform of talk
بدا في التَّحَدُّث أمام الحُضور	to take the floor
مَحْضَر الجَلْسة	session minutes
حَلْقة نِقاش	discussion circle
مُداخَلة	intervention

مُنتَدى، مُنْتدَيات	forum
مُؤتَمر، ـات	conference
نَدْوة، نَدَوات	panel
مُحادَثات	talks, discussions
مُناقَشات	discussions
مُشاوَرات	consultations
أجرى مُحادَثات	to hold talks
عقد يعقِد عَقْد مُحادَثات	to convene talks
مُحادَثات تَحْضيريّة	preparatory talks
مُحادَثات تَمْهيديّة	preliminary talks
إجْتِماعات تَمْهيديّة \ تَحضيريّة	preparatory meetings
جَلْسة إفْتَتاحيّة	opening session
جَلْسة خِتاميّة	closing session
مُحادَثات رَفيعة المُستَوى	high-level talks
مُحادَثات جادّة	serious talks
مُحادَثات بَنّاءة	constructive discussions

تَرْحيب بالمُحادَثات	welcoming the talks
رَفْض المُحادَثات	rejection of talks
مُقاطَعة المُحادَثات	interruption of talks
جَوْلة مُحادَثات	round of talks
فَتْح فَصْل جَديد مِن المُحادَثات	opening a new chapter of talks
إنْفِراج في المُحادَثات	breakthrough in talks
تَعَثُّر المُحادَثات	stalemate in talks
تَعْليق المُحادَثات	suspension of talks
إسْتِئْناف المُحادَثات	resumption of talks
إسْتِكمال المُحادَثات	conclusion of talks
تَقَدُّم في المُحادَثات	progress in talks
فَشَل المُحادَثات	failure of talks
نَجاح المُحادَثات	success of talks
إخْتَتَم المُحادَثات	to conclude talks
نَتائج المُحادَثات	talks outcomes/ results

achievement of concrete results   تَحْقيق نَتائِج مَلْمُوسة

EU accession talks   مُحادَثات الإنْضِمام للاتِّحاد الأوروبّيّ

formalities   شَكْليّات \ رَسْميّات

7. TREATIES & AGREEMENTS

اِتِّفاق \ اِتِّفاقِيّة، ـات	agreement/treaty
مُعاهَدة، ـات	treaty/convention
عَقْد، عُقود	contract
وَثيقة، وَثائِق	document/deed
مُستند، ـات	instrument
تَفاهُم، ـات	accord/entente
مِيثاق، مَواثيق	charter
إعلان، ـات	declaration
عقَّد يعقِد عَقْد \ أَبْرم	to conclude (a pact/agreement)
وقَّع	to sign
وقَّع بِالأَحْرُف الأُولى	to initial
تَوَصَّل إلى	to reach
إنْتَهى إلى	to arrive at
إنْضَمّ إلى	to accede to
إشْتَرَك في	to be a part of

تَمَسَّك بـ	to hold to
راعَى	to observe/heed
أعاد النَظَر في	to revise
عَدَّل	to amend
أنْهَى	to terminate
خرق يخرِق خَرْق	to breach
إنْسَحَب من	to withdraw
نقَض ينقُض نَقْض	to violate
ألْغَى	to annul
نَفَّذ	to implement
طَبَّق قَلْبًا وقالِبًا	to apply in letter and spirit
سرَى يَسري سَرَيان	to enter into force
صَدَّق على	to ratify
سَجَّل	to register
إحْتَرَم	to respect
تَقَيَّد بِ	to be bound by/comply with
ثُنائيّ	bilateral

مُتَعدِّد الأطُراف multilateral

شَفَويّ verbal

فَرْعيّ subsidiary

جُزْئيّ partial

تَكْميليّ supplementary

ضِمْنيّ implied

مُعاهَدة تَحالُف treaty of alliance

مُعاهَدة الدِّفاع المُشْتَرَك treaty of mutual defence

مُعاهَدة هُدْنة armistice treaty

مُعاهَدة سلام \ صُلْح peace accord/treaty

مُعاهَدة جماعيّة collective treaty

مُعاهَدة تَسْليم المُجْرمين extradition treaty

مُعاهَدة قُنصُليّة consular treaty

مُعاهَدة تِجاريّة commercial treaty

مُعاهَدة حُسْن الجِوار treaty of good neighbourhood

مُعاهَدة ضَمان treaty of guarantee

مُعاهَدة إستِقْلال	independence treaty
مُعاهَدة حِياد	treaty of neutrality
مُعاهَدة عَدَم إعْتِداء	non-aggression treaty
مُعاهَدة تَحْكيم	arbitration treaty
مُسَوَّدة	draft
صِياغة	wording
ديباجة	preamble
بَنْد، بُنود	clause
بَنْد إضافيّ	additional clause
بَنْد غامِض	ambiguous clause
بَنْد خَفِيّ	hidden clause
بَنْد خِتاميّ	final clause
تَعْديل أَخْطاء الصِّياغة	amendment of drafting errors
مُلْحَق، -ات \ مَلاحِق	annex
لُغات المُعاهَدة	treaty languages
شُروط المُعاهَدة	treaty terms
تَبادُل الوَثائِق	document exchange

نُسْخة مُصَدَّقة	certified copy
إعْتمد نَصّ المُعاهَدة	to adopt/sanction the treaty text
نشر ينشُر نَشْر	to publish
طَبَّق	to apply
فَسَّر	to interpret
اتِّفاقِيّة لُنْدُن	London Convention
اتِّفاقِيّة سايكُس بيكو	Sykes-Picot Agreement
اتِّفاقِيّة لَوْزان	Lausanne Convention
اتِّفاقِيّة أوسْلو	Oslo Agreement/ Oslo Accords
اتِّفاقِيّة باريس لِمُكافَحة تَغَيُّر المَناخ	Paris Convention on Climate Change
اتِّفاقِيّة حَظْر الأَسْلِحة الكيميائِيّة	Chemical Weapons Convention
اتِّفاقِيّة التِّجارة الحُرّة	Free Trade Agreement
الإعْلان العالَميّ لِحُقوق الإنْسان	Universal Declaration of Human Rights
مُعاهَدة تورْدَسيلاس	Treaty of Tordesillas

مُعاهَدة سَلام وَسْتْفاليا	Peace of Westphalia
مُعاهَدة باريس	Treaty of Paris
مُؤْتَمَر فيينا	Congress of Vienna
مُعاهَدة فَرْساي	Treaty of Versailles
مُعاهَدة جِنيف للسَّلام	Geneva Peace Convention
اِتِّفاقيّة فيينا لِلعَلاقات الدِّبْلوماسيّة والقُنْصُلِيّة	Vienna Convention on Diplomatic and Consular Relations
اِتِّفاقيّة جِنيف	Geneva Convention
اِتِّفاقيّة لاهاي	Hague Convention
حِلْف وارْسو	Warsaw Pact
مُعاهَدة كامْب ديفيد (للسَّلام)	Camp David Accords
مُعاهَدة الحَدّ من إِنْتِشار الأَسْلِحة النَوويّة	Treaty on the Non-Proliferation of Nuclear Weapons

8. CONFLICT RESOLUTION & DEFENCE

صِراع، ـات	conflict
مَنْع نُشوب صِراع	conflict prevention
إثارة صِراع	provoking conflict
زيادة حِدّة الصِّراع	increasing the intensity of the conflict
صِراع مُسَلَّح	armed conflict
صِراع سياسيّ	political conflict
نِزاع قانونيّ	legal dispute
صِراع يَتَّسِم بالعُنْف	violent conflict
الصِّراع العربيّ الإسرائيليّ	Arab–Israeli Conflict
سَبَب الصِّراع	cause of conflict
في حالة أيّ صِراع	in the event of any conflict
فَضّ النِّزاعات	conflict resolution
آلية فَضّ النِّزاعات	conflict resolution mechanism
أطْراف النِّزاع	parties to the conflict

التَّوَسُّط في النِّزاع	conflict mediation
خِلاف، ـات	dispute
تَسوية الخِلافات	dispute settlement
تَوافُق	compatibility
مُصالَحة	conciliation
مَساعٍ حَميدة	good offices
نَهْج تَصالُحيّ	conciliatory approach
مَصالِح مُشتَرَكة	common interests
تَهِدِئة الأوضاع	de-escalation
جُهود الوساطة	intercession efforts
مُفاوَضات الوساطة	intercession negotiations
عَرْض الوساطة	intercession offer
تَوصَّل إلى حَلّ وَسَط	to reach a compromise
صيغة التَّسْوية	compromise formula
القانون الدّوَليّ	international law
سيادة القانون	rule of law

تَسْوية قَضائيّة لِمُنازَعات	judicial settlement of disputes
وَقْف إطْلاق النار	ceasefire
تَجْريد مِن السِّلاح	disarmament/demilitarisation
إبادة جَماعيّة	genocide
جريمة الحَرْب، جَرائِم الحَرْب	war crime
مَجْزَرة، مَجازِر	massacre
تَطْهير عِرْقيّ	ethnic cleansing
إرْهاب	terrorism
هُجوم إرْهابيّ	terrorist attack
عَسْكَريّ	military
المُؤَسَّسة العَسْكَريّة	the military
وُجود عَسْكَريّ	military presence
تَدَخُّل عَسْكَريّ	military intervention
مواجَهة عَسْكَريّة	military confrontation
تَحرُّك عَسْكَريّ	military movement
عَمَليّات عَسْكَريّة مُشْتَرَكة	joint military exercises

حَرْب، حُروب	war (Arabic fem.)
حَرْب أَهْليّة	civil war
حَرْب بِالوَكالة	proxy war
حَرْب عِصابات	guerilla war
حَرْب عادِلة	just war
في حالةِ الحَرْب	at war
مَسْرَح الحَرْب	theatre of war
مِيدان العَمَليّات	field of operations
مِيليشيا، مِيليشيات	militia
القُوّات المُسَلَّحة	the armed forces
القُوّات الجَوّيّة	the air force
البَحْريّة	the navy
جَيْش، جُيوش	army
المُشاة	the infantry (Arabic pl.)
قُوّات بَرّيّة	ground forces
قُوّة مُتَعَدِّدة الجِنْسيّات	multinational force
قُوّات حِفْظِ السَّلام	peacekeeping forces
قُوّات تَحالُف	coalition forces

قُوّة دِفاعيّة	defence force
قُوّة رَدْع	deterrent force
قُوّة هُجوميّة ضاربة	strike force
قُوّة خَفيفة	light/mobile task force
قُوّات اِحْتياطيّة	reserves
قُوّات قِتاليّة	combat troops
رُكْن، أَرْكان	military staff
جُنْديّ، جُنود	soldier
مَدَنيّ، -ون	civilian
بَحّار، -ون \ بَحّارة	sailor
جُنْديّ مُشاةِ البَحْريّة	marine
طَيّار، -ون	airman, pilot
مِظَلّيّ، -ون	paratrooper
قانِص، قُنّاص	sniper
قُوّة خاصّة	commando, special troop
بَطَل، أَبْطال	hero
مُنْشَقّ، -ون	defector

شارِد، شَوارِد \ شُرُد	deserter
أسير، أسْرَى	captive
أسير حَرْب، أسْرَى حَرْب	prisoner of war (POW)
تَبادُل الأسْرَى	prisoner swap
إرْهابيّ، ـون	terrorist
مُجاهِد، ـون	jihadist/holy warrior
مُجْرِم حَرْب، مُجْرِمو حَرْب	war criminal
لِواء، ألْوية	general/flag
رَئيس الأرْكان	Chief of Staff
رُتْبة، رُتَب	rank/grade
سِرْب، أسْراب	squadron
كَتيبة، كَتائِب	battalion/brigade
وَحْدة، وَحَدات	(military) unit
فَصيلة، فَصائِل	cell/squad
فَصيلة الإعْدام	execution squad/ firing squad
دَوْريّة، ـات	patrol

سِلاح، أَسْلِحة	weapon
أَسْلِحة خَفيفة \ صَغيرة	small arms
ذَخيرة	ammunition
مَظَلّة، ـات	parachute
تَرْسانة، ـات	arsenal
أَسْلِحة نَوَويّة	nuclear weapons
رَدْع نَوَويّ	nuclear deterrent
أَسْلِحة ذَكِيّة	precision weapons
سِباق تَسَلُّح	arms race
أَسْلِحة الدَمارِ الشامِل	weapons of mass destruction (WMD)
صاروخ، صَواريخ	missile, rocket
صاروخ مُضادّ لِلطّائِرات	anti-aircraft missile
صاروخ تَمْويهيّ	decoy missile
صاروخ طَوّاف	cruise missile
صاروخ سَطْح - جَوّ	surface-to-air missile
صاروخ بَعيد \ قَصير المَدَى	long-/short-range missile

قَذيفة عابِرة لِلقارّات	intercontinental ballistic missile
قاذِفة الصَواريخ	rocket/missile launcher
نَسيفة، نَسائِف	torpedo
قُنْبُلة، قَنابِل	bomb
أداة تَفْجير	explosive device
مُتَفَجِّرات	explosives
قُنْبُلة يَدَويّة	hand grenade
قُنْبُلة نَوَويّة	nuclear bomb
قُنْبُلة ذَرّيّة	atomic bomb
قُنْبُلة عُنْقوديّة	cluster bomb
قَذيفة هاوُن، قَذائِف هاوُن	mortar bomb
لَغَم \ لُغْم، ألْغام	mine
رَصاصة، ـات \ رَصاص	bullet
مِدْفَع، مَدافِع	gun
مُسَدَّس، ـات	revolver
مِدْفَع رَشّاش	machine gun

رَشّاش قَصير	sub-machine gun
بُنْدُقِيّة آليّة	automatic rifle
سِلاح قَذّافيّ	ballistic weapon
قِطْعة مِدْفَعيّة	(piece of) artillery
قَصْف مِدْفَعيّ	artillery fire
قَصْف صاروخيّ	rocket fire
شَظايا	shrapnel (Arabic pl.)
إشْعاع	radiation
اِنْفِجار \ تَفْجير، ـات	explosion
قَصْف	bombardment, shelling
قَصْف دَقيق \ ذَكيّ	precision bombing
ضَرْبة وِقائيّة	preemptive strike
إسْتِخْدام القُوّة	use of force
غِطاء جَوّيّ	air cover
دِفاعات جَوّيّة	air defences
مِنْطَقة حَظْر جَوّيّ	no-fly zone
مِنْطَقة مَنْزوعة السِّلاح	demilitarised zone

مِنْطَقة القِتال	combat zone
ناقِلة جُنود مُدَرَّعة	armoured personnel carrier
دَبّابة، ـات	tank
طائِرة مِرْوَحيّة \ هَليكوبْتَر	helicopter
حامِلة طائِرات	aircraft carrier
طائِرة مُقاتِلة	fighter aircraft
طائِرة بِدونَ طَيّار	drone
مُدَمِّرة، ـات	destroyer
سَفينة حَرْبيّة، سُفُن حَرْبيّة	warship
بارِجة، بَوارِج	frigate
زَوْرَق حَرْبيّ، زَوارِق حَرْبيّة	gunboat
غَوّاصة	submarine
أُسْطول، أَساطيل	fleet
قَاعِدة عَسْكَريّة، قَواعِد عَسْكَريّة	military base
مَقَرّ، مَقارّ	headquarters (HQ)

مَوْقِع إِسْتراتيجيّ، strategic position
مَواقِع إِسْتراتيجيّة

إِنْتِشار الأَسْلِحة nuclear proliferation
النَوَويّة

عَدَم الإِنْتِشار النَوَويّ nuclear non-
    proliferation

جِهاز طَرْد مَرْكَزيّ centrifugal system

تَخْصيب اليورانيوم enrichment of uranium

مُناوَرة، ـات manoeuvre

إِسْتِطْلاع reconnaissance

إِسْتِعْراض \ عَرْض parade

مَعْرَكة، مَعارِك battle

خَطَر، أَخْطار \ danger
مَخاطِر

أَمْن safety

دَرْع بَشَريّ، دُروع human shield
بَشَريّة

غارة، ـات raid

هُجوم بَرّيّ ground offensive

هُجوم بَرْمائيّ amphibious attack

هُجوم مُسَلَّح عَلَى	armed attack on
هُجوم مُضادّ	counter attack
كَمين، كَمائِن	ambush
تَكْتيكات	tactics
اِعْتِداءات عَلى	aggressions against
رَدّ اِنْتِقاميّ عَلى	revenge for
في وَضْع اِسْتِعْداد لِ	in a state of readiness for
مُنْتَشِر	deployed
عُدْوانيّ \ عَدائيّ	hostile
اِنْعِكاسات \ عَواقِب	repercussions
حشد يحشِد حَشْد	to mobilise, call up
حشَّد	to amass (especially troops)
جَنَّد	to draft, conscript
اِسْتَدْعَى	to call up
عَزَّز	to reinforce
نشر ينشُر نَشْر	to deploy
تَفَقَّد	to inspect
فَجَّر	to explode (transitive verb)

تَفَجَّر	to explode (intransitive verb)
دَمَّر \ هَدَّم	to destroy
أباد \ أفْنَى	to annihilate
قضَى يقضي قَضاء عَلى تَمَرُّد	to put down a revolt
أُسْتُشْهِد	to be martyred (Arabic passive)
أُصيبَ بِجُروح خَطيرة \ طَفيفة	to suffer serious/minor injuries (Arabic passive)
هجم يهجُم هُجوم عَلى	to attack
غزا يَغزو غَزْو	to invade, raid
أعْلَن الحَرْب	to declare war
شنّ يشُنّ شَنّ هُجوماً \ حَمْلةً	to launch an attack/campaign
أطْلَق	to launch (missile, torpedo, etc.)
إقْتَحَم	to storm
تَسَلَّل إلى	to infiltrate
حاصَر	to besiege, surround

فتح يِفتَح فَتْح النّار \ أَطلَق النّار	to open fire
تَبادَل إطْلاق النّار	to exchange fire
دافَع عَن	to defend
حمى يحمي حِماية مِن	to protect against
إنْسَحَب	to withdraw (intransitive verb)
جلا يجلو جَلاء عَن	to evacuate (intransitive verb)
أَجْلى	to evacuate (transitive verb)
إسْتَسْلَم	to surrender
أَطْلَق	to free
أَطلَق سَراحَهُ	to set free
إسْتَأْنَف القِتال	to resume fighting
قاوَم	to resist
خَطَّط	to plan
تَآمَر	to plot
إسْتَهْدَف	to target

نصب ينصُب نَصْب to erect road blocks
حَواجِز عَلَى الطُرُق

فرض يفرُض فَرْض to impose a cordon/
حِصاراً عَلَى blockade on

إنْدَلَع to break out (war)

إحْتَلّ to occupy

إخْتَرَق الحُدود to cross the border(s)

تَسَلَّل خَلْف الحُدود to slip across the border

قَدَّر حَجْمَ القُوّات to estimate the strength of
forces

إسْتَخْلَص المعلومات to debrief

9. CIVIL SOCIETY & HUMAN RIGHTS

المُجْتَمَع المَدَنيّ	civil society
مُؤَسَّسة المُجْتَمَع المَدَنيّ	civil society organisation (CSO)
جَمْعيّة أَهْليّة	civil society association
مُنَظَّمة غَيْر حُكوميّة	non-governmental organisation (NGO)
العَقْد الإجْتِماعيّ	the social contract
غَيْر رِبْحيّ	non-profit
تَعْزيز مُشارَكة المُجْتَمَع المَدَنيّ في	fostering civil society participation in
عَمَليّات صُنْع القَرار	decision-making processes
إسْهامات المُجْتَمَع المَدَنيّ	contributions of civil society
تَعْزيز الدّيموقْراطيّة	strengthening democracy
تَنْمية مُسْتَدامة	sustainable development
تَمْكين المُجْتَمَع المَدَنيّ	empowerment of civil society

عَمَل تَطَوُّعيّ — volunteerism

تَقْديم الخِدْمات — service delivery

إعْتِبارات أَخْلاقيّة — ethical considerations

كفل يكْفُل كَفْل حُرّيّة التَعْبير — to guarantee freedom of speech

حُقوق الإنْسان — human rights

التَّمَتُّع بِالحُقوق — enjoyment of rights

ضَمان لِحُقوق الإنْسان — guarantee of human rights

جَمْعيّة حُقوق الإنْسان — human rights association

عَدالة — justice

مُساواة — equality

إحْتِرام الكَرامة الإنْسانيّة — respect for human dignity

الإعْلان العالَميّ لِحُقوق الإنْسان — Universal Declaration of Human Rights

بَرْنامَج الأُمَم المُتَّحِدة لِحُقوق الإنْسان — United Nations Human Rights Programme

المُفَوَّض السامي لِحُقوق الإنْسان — United Nations High Commissioner for Human Rights

مَعايير دَوليّة	international standards
إنْتِهاكات حُقوق الإنْسان	human rights violations
جَرائم ضِدّ الإنْسانيّة	crimes against humanity
حالة حُقوق الإنْسان	human rights situation
إتّفاقيّة القَضاء على جَميع أشْكال التَمْييز ضِدّ المَرْأة	Convention on the Elimination of All Forms of Discrimination against Women
مُكافَحة كافّة أشْكال التَمْييز	combating all forms of discrimination
حُقوق الأقَلّيّات	minority rights
حُقوق اللّاجِئِين	refugee rights
المَبادِئ الأساسيّة لِمُعامَلة السُجَناء	Basic Principles for the Treatment of Prisoners
حُقوق مَدنيّة	civil rights
حَمَى يحمي حِماية	to protect
حَسَّن	to improve
أمَّن	to safeguard
رصد يرصُد رَصْد	to observe

راقَب   to monitor

وَثَّق   to document

كافَح   to combat

10. GLOBALISATION & ECONOMIC DEVELOPMENT

عَوْلَمة	globalisation
عَوْلَمة سِياسيّة	political globalisation
عَوْلَمة اِقْتِصاديّة	economic globalisation
عَوْلَمة ثَقافيّة	cultural globalisation
أَصْل العَوْلَمة	origin of globalisation
خَصائِص العَوْلَمة	characteristics of globalisation
خُصوصيّة ثَقافيّة	cultural particularity
نِسْبيّة ثَقافيّة	cultural relativism
مَخاطِر العَوْلَمة	perils of globalisation
مُناهِض لِلعَوْلَمة	anti-globalisation
مُواطِن عَوْلَميّ	globalised citizen
قَرْية كَوْنيّة	global village
مُجْتَمَع المَعْلومات العالَميّ	global information society
تِجارة عابِرة للحُدود	trans-national trade

شَركات مُتَعَدِّدة الجِنْسِيّات	multinational corporations
تَعاوُن دَوليّ	international cooperation
إزالة \ رَفْع الحَواجِز الجُمْرُكيّة	abolishing/lifting tariff barriers
وَسائِل الإتِّصالات	means of communication
ثَورة الإتِّصالات	communications revolution
تَنْمية إقْتِصاديّة	economic development
تَنْمية بَشَريّة	human development
تَنْمية مُسْتدامة	sustainable development
تَمْويل	financing
أهْداف إنْمائيّة	development objectives
نُمو إقْتِصاديّ	economic growth
حَدّ مِن الفَقْر	poverty reduction
تَحَسُّن المُسْتَوى المَعيشيّ	enhancement in living standard
رَخاء ورَفاهيّة	prosperity and well-being
تَقَدُّم	progress
تَخَلُّف	backwardness

بُلْدان نامية	developing countries
مُعَدَّلات النُّمو الإقْتِصاديّ	economic growth rates
إقْتِصاد السّوق الحُرّة	free market economy
أزْمة ماليّة عالَميّة	international financial crisis
تَكَيُّف	adjustment
إعادة الهَيْكلة	restructuring
خُطَط التَّنْمية	development plans
قِطاع الأَعْمال	business sector
تَبادُل تِجاريّ	commercial exchange/trading

INDEX

treaty, 8
  peace treaty, 8, 57
  treaty terms, 60
  commercial treaty, 59
  collective treaty, 59
  extradition treaty,
    59
tribalism, 12
truce, 7
trusteeship, 15

UNDFW (United
    Nations
    Development
    Fund for
    Women), 31
UNHCR (United
    Nations High
    Commission for
    Human Rights),
    31
UNHCR (United
    Nations Refugee
    Agency), 31
UNPF (United Nations
    Population Fund),
    30
UNRWA (United
    Nations Relief
    and Works
    Agency for
    Palestine
    Refugees), 31

unity, 45
utopianism, 12

victory, 47
vote, 39
  vote of confidence,
    42
  vote of no-
    confidence, 42

war, 66
  civil war, 66
  guerilla war, 66
  prisoner of war, 68
  proxy war, 66
  war crime, 65
  war criminal, 68
Warsaw Pact, 62
weapon, 69
  ballistic weapon, 71
  nuclear weapons, 69
  weapon of mass
    destruction, 69
World Bank, 29
World Food
    Programme
    (WFP), 30
World Health
    Organization
    (WHO), 30
World Trade
    Organization
    (WTO), 30